What Did You Just Say?

True Quotes

From

Real Insurance Adjusters

By

ANNA MISS

This book contains quotes documented during actual auto insurance settlements. No names have been used in order to protect the not so innocent perpetrators.

What Did You Just Say?

Efi Loo Publishing, Inc.

efiloopublishing@gmail.com

First paperback edition.

ISBN-13: 978-0615918334 (Efi Loo Publishing, Inc.)

ISBN-10: 0615918336

EFI LOO PUBLISHING

DEDICATION

To the many people in my life who have helped me to find humor in situations that often brought tears.

EPIGRAPH

During my twenty-plus years working in the auto insurance industry I collected a vast array of unique and hilarious quotes blurted out by fellow peers; including my own, during the heated debate of a negotiation.

Whether you're in the process of settling a claim with an indifferent insurance agent or an insurance adjuster looking for that perfect one-line zinger to settle a difficult claim, then *What Did You Just Say?* will be sure to equip you with the right words to help you on your journey into the mysterious world of insurance negotiations.

And for the rest, you never know, your day may come.

"Live a little, love a lot and always find time to laugh."
Anna Miss

.

Caution: The following contents may result in spontaneous laughter. Side effects could include, but are not limited to; a sudden onset of crying, the unexplained release of an empty bladder or an overwhelming sensation of disappointment the moment you realize, why didn't I think to say that?

Choose wisely on where you decide to read, *What Did You Just Say?*

"When you're not on drugs, call me back and we'll settle your claim."

"I have an appraiser who, in essence, is my eyes and ears."

"I haven't been able to break the time continuum, but I'm trying."

"If you call me a liar one more time, I will hang up on you."

"Your idle threats do not impress me."

"I am not here to be liked!"

"We do have your best interest at heart."

"If you overnight the check, we will overnight the payment to the check."

"Dadgumit, where is it?"

"I am disappointed and disillusioned that we have been unable to reach an acceptable resolution in this debacle."

"I have feelings too. I know sometimes it doesn't seem that way, but I do."

"I can write down in chapter and verse what your wife states were in the publications."

"We are agreeing to disagree."

"We don't use any book values. You and I could get together and call it your last name and my last name book and we still wouldn't consider it."

"We are not a bank!"

"It's like another twig on a branch."

"Let the rest of the world battle their own fight."

"You wouldn't want to see me naked … I'll scare the shit out of you!"

"I have nothing to tell you. No use getting agitated."

"I will slip that rental away as quickly as he can say hallelujah!"

"Are you going to pay my salary for keeping me on the phone?"

"So, if that office burnt down you couldn't function?"

"Okay, what is your last name … do you have a last name?"

"Sometimes, even a blind squirrel finds a nut."

"It's a crime that we have to do business with you!"

"I don't owe you a penny more or a penny less."

"Are you gonna let me finish?"

"Maybe you can tell me who is handling this claim, so I don't have to meet the whole company."

"All I know is that the first and second year in a lease is horrendous!"

"We are not your enemy."

"She's got a misapprehension about who the hell she is."

"Let's cut all this out. C'mon, I'm trying to help you."

"I feel for you ... I really do."

"I'm on your side here … okay?"

"I have the advantage, because I have the educated know how."

"Regardless if we are in Ohio or Florida, you should feel like we're right down the street from you."

"This relationship has broken down to where I am putting everything into writing. Now, you will do the same."

"I'm sorry it had to happen this way, but at least you're back on the road!"

"Ma'am, did you call to yell at me or get the status of your claim?"

"This country's defense is not dependent upon the wiring of your car."

"I'm not going to talk to you any longer, because you don't know what you're talking about."

"I am in a precarious position. I'm going to speak with you frankly ... that means, I am going to speak with you off the record and if you bring it up again and somebody asks me ... I will tell them, I don't know what you are talking about."

"Okay, we've done this for 75 years and have not had a problem."

"When you file a claim, you can't just pick parts of the claim that you want to file."

"You got to be careful, because he pees all over the place ... he only gets a little drink."

"We are going around the long way here to get across the street."

"Are you awake?"

"Well, don't ask if you already know."

"Wait a minute ... let me just prove a point!"

"You are not going to hold me to a higher standard than the law holds you to."

"I have forgotten more than you'll ever know!"

"I'm sending you a check today and I'm not talking to you anymore!"

"I don't know how to explain it, because we have already told you ten million times."

"You don't have to send me a letter and we don't have to talk anymore."

"You've got to promise me that you will NEVER call me again, and I will split the mileage with you!"

"I am not your son!"

"You're entitled to your opinion and I am entitled to the facts ... and you don't have to like it."

"Don't worry … if it doesn't get done today, it won't get done tomorrow."

"Those who know nothing have all the answers."

"It's the squeaky wheel that gets the oil."

"Do I have to be on the phone while you talk to yourself or do you have any questions for me?"

"I wish I could shut up, too, but I can't."

"Religion has nothing to do with the value of your vehicle."

"No, you didn't compromise. You started at $2,000 and you're still at $2,000."

"Let me tell you something ... you're going to get a good education here today."

"Wait a minute ... you're talking to a motorcycle guy, so let's be careful."

"I am not smarter than everyone else. Everyone else is dumber than me."

"My final offer, just because it's a busy day. I'll split the difference with you."

"What did you say? You're not my mama?"

"Duly noted … my bad."

"You are a spineless jellyfish."

"A 1994 Volvo doesn't generate much interest in the market place."

"The interior of your car wouldn't make a good dog bed."

And, the absolute zinger…

"I'm sorry that you were almost killed last week, but that doesn't add to the value of your truck."

"A 1994 Volvo doesn't generate much interest in the market place."

Now that you are equipped with the ultimate one-liners and know how to intelligently respond, happy claim settling!

The End

"The interior of your car wouldn't make a good dog bed."

And, the absolute zinger…

"I'm sorry that you were almost killed last week, but that doesn't add to the value of your truck."

Now that you are equipped with the ultimate one-liners and know how to intelligently respond, happy claim settling!

The End

www.ingramcontent.com/pod-product-compliance
Lightning Source LLC
Chambersburg PA
CBHW060650030426
42337CB00017B/2539